# HEART SHAPED ROCKS

## Don't Die Without Me

# HEART SHAPED ROCKS

## Don't Die Without Me

Misty VanderWeele

Heart Shaped Rocks, Don't Die Without Me

**ISBN 978-0-9893247-1-7**

Cover Design: Misty Vanderweele

www.MistyVanderweele.com

Interior Design ©2014 by BookDesignTemplates.com

Cover Photograph by Jay Johnson of Healing Life Touch Photography

*To my favorite daughter. It's an honor to be your mother and your friend. I look forward to all our "NEXT" adventures together.*

# Acknowledgements

Heart Shaped Rocks wouldn't have come to light without you, Jenna. You have been through it all, perhaps not unscathed but an amazing, fun, and deeply loving part of my life. Thank you, my darling daughter. I couldn't get through grieving your brother or keep being the advocate I am for Duchenne without you right here by my side. You've had to witness some pretty dark moments of mine, and while I see the look of concern you have for me what I feel the most is your undying love. The grace you exemplify and the sincerity you possess are true inspiration for me. You are the best daughter anyone could ever ask for.

My next thank you goes out to the wonderful man I married, Glen. Your support and personal strength have helped me bring Heart Shaped Rocks from just a thought in my mind to an actual physical piece of our history. It's an honor to be raising Jenna with you. Thank you my all of the above.

A huge thank you goes to Suus VanderWeele, my beloved mother-in-law. The genuine friendship, love, and support you extend to me over and over are deeply felt. All the Tea Times mean so much to me, and I know Jenna feels the same way about her grandma.

During a particularly hard grieving day, coupled with a lot of negativity being dumped on me, I was feeling very down. I felt like just giving up being an advocate. I was walking around Walgreens when a lady named Tammy came up to me and asked if I was Misty VanderWeele. I said yes, and she went on to tell me with tears in her eyes that she had lost her own brother to Duchenne years ago and that all I do for Duchenne truly matters. Thank you, Tammy, for being the message I so needed to hear at that moment. Later that day I went on and pre-launched this book.

To Kelley Caraway, I love our decade and a half of friendship. Your genuine feelings for me are greatly received and warmly returned. Our friendship deeply humbles me. You've seen me at my best and my worst and you still love me anyway. I look forward to the next decade of our lives.

Autumn Tweedy, distance must make the heart grow fonder. Either that or I just miss you like nuts! Thank you for your love and encouragement to be the best me that I can be. Sis, you see me how I need to see me. xoxoxo

Lucia, every once in a while you re-cross paths with people like it is all part of life's plan. How ironic that I was your nanny, helping to take care of you, and now you are taking care of my writing with your editing. Thank you for the amazing job you've done on Heart Shaped Rocks. You helped polish Jenna's story into a shiny penny with professionalism, while holding nothing back. I always knew you were going to turn out to be an incredible individual. We will be working together again soon.

Awww, next is the beautiful, loving Kathleen Jones. I can't express enough how much the true friendship you bestow upon Jenna and my family means to me. Thank you for being there for Jenna when she needed you the most all those years ago, and even more recently after we lost Luke. The love, PEACE, and support you give are treasured by her just as much as me.

Before you jump into reading Heart Shaped Rocks I want to thank each and every person who has sought me out to see how I am doing. Thank you for taking the time out of your day to connect, ask questions, and share with me. One day I hope to meet you all in person.

# Introduction

Heart Shaped Rocks is a story in progress. It is my daughter Jenna's story, a living story which unfolds little by little every day. You see, Jenna, like tens of thousands of other siblings, has spent her first 14 years on this planet knowing that her brother could die at any moment from complications of Duchenne Muscular Dystrophy.

Duchenne Muscular Dystrophy, or simply Duchenne or DMD as it is commonly referred to, is the most common form of muscular dystrophy. It is a muscle wasting disease which mainly affects boys, although girls can be diagnosed with it too. Its victims, like my son Luke, are born seemingly healthy, but as time goes on and the disease progresses, the body's muscles get thinner and weaker, eventually rendering the child unable to walk. By the age of 10 or 12 a Duchenne child must use an electric wheelchair for mobility. A manual wheelchair isn't practical since he is usually too weak to propel himself. At the same time Duchenne takes away lower body strength, it starts affecting upper body strength, eventually destroying the heart and lungs which results in premature death in young adulthood, usually by the late teens or mid-twenties.

When Jenna was born, her brother, Luke, was able to hold and feed her. In her toddler years she rode on the back of his electric wheelchair. By the time she was in elementary school, Luke was not able to lift his arms to hug her or even give her a brotherly slug in the arm. Although Jenna's story of life as a Duchenne sibling is heartbreaking, I want you to know that like my first book, *In Your Face Duchenne Muscular Dystrophy, All Pain...All GLORY!,* this book is about making the very most out of what life throws at you while looking for those synchronistic signs and Aha moments that teach you that life is meant to be lived on purpose. This time, instead of telling the story of my son's battle with DMD, my intention is to honor my daughter's life as she watches how much Duchenne takes from her brother, while at the same time benefiting from all that it gives in terms of passion, maturity, and strength of character.

As her mother, it's an honor to witness the transformation of a young girl into the young woman Jenna is becoming. She has so much to offer this world. Just wait until you read how on purpose and full of love for life Jenna is and how Duchenne has molded her. Living in the face of uncertainty has helped her develop into a young lady submerged in love for life, compassion, and the example of living grace. She gives her heart gently, but full on. I am sure you'll fall in love with her one heart shaped rock at a time.

Heart Shaped Rocks follows my son, Luke's, progression with Duchenne starting with my pregnancy with Jenna, all the way to the present day with Jenna now being 14 years old. It details her journey as Duchenne ravages her brother's body and then takes his life. You will be moved by Jenna over and over as you read about the love they shared. But first let me give you some background with which to lay out her story.

As a Duchenne carrier, I have a 50% chance of having a child born with Duchenne. And as I mentioned earlier, Duchenne mostly affects boys but girls can have it too (although that's very rare). So when my son was diagnosed back in 1994 I had decided there would be no more children for me. At that time I had just started a relationship with my now husband Glen and we decided that having one child would be enough for both of us. Besides, I knew what was to come in the future and I wasn't too sure I wanted to put this kind of grief into another person's life, let alone another child. However, life had a surprise in store for us.

That surprise was Jenna.

Although having another child wasn't planned and often left me worried about the future, I knew it was supposed to be or it wouldn't be happening in the first place. There are almost 8 years between Luke and Jenna. This means their sibling relationship is unique. Luke was the typical protective big brother, but as time went on and Luke started losing more of his physical ability, Jenna would step in and be his hands, arms, and feet. They would roam the fields of the farm where we live, Jenna his photographer and he the director. She would sit long hours and watch him play video games and fetch his water when he asked. Their mutual admiration was always felt. They would squabble now and again, but what siblings don't? Watching their interaction with each other always brought me such joy, with a little sadness around the edges if I thought about a future without Luke in it and how that would affect Jenna.

During the writing of this book, we laid Jenna's brother, to rest in a beautiful cemetery with the view of what Luke referred to as his mountains. Currently, I live, work and play with my daughter, Jenna, and my husband, Glen, on his family's vegetable farm here in Alaska. It's an incredible lifestyle to be a part of, with all the fresh air, vegetables and scenery. Most people don't know but Alaska got started with agriculture back in 1935 through President Roosevelt's resettlement program. Although many farms are not in operation anymore, there are a handful of farmers left. Some of us are lobbying for Alaska to be a selfsustainable state. We live in a vast valley surrounded by mountains and glaciers. Our home in particular has an incredible view and numerous fields to roam, which we enjoy frequently. It's an incredible place to raise a family and grow a happy life. It's one of many things I am in awe of; I feel deeply grateful to get to live here and I embrace all that this home-spun family-farm lifestyle has to offer.

So what does Heart Shaped Rocks have to do with living in the face of Duchenne? Well, you will learn just that as you continue to turn the pages of this book.

# Preface

What a fortunate teacher I am that Jenna Vanderweele and her family came into my life. I feel incredibly honored to be a contributing member of this book about such a wonderful kid.

Jenna and I first met in the spring quarter of her 3rd grade year when I occasionally helped out in her reading class. She was quick, funny and very direct! I learned soon after that Jenna was often worried about her older brother Luke's health. She carried this around in the most heartfelt way, was leery about sharing this news with just anyone and would sometimes break down into tears if pushed too far. She was still working through so much of the world happening around her. When the school year ended I hoped that our paths would cross again. And, to my good fortune, they did!

The following fall, Jenna was placed in my 4th grade classroom! I've always enjoyed Jenna and was so pleased we would be continuing our learning together. We had a great time that year, teaching one another about love, light, PEACE and laughter! When I moved up to teach 5th grade the following year I was allowed to take a few kids with me. Jenna was on the list! This was wonderful for us both as I grew closer to her mom, met her Dad and of course, her brother, Luke.

Luke's health was a main priority with Jenna and her family, which was all encompassing for them. When Luke was doing well, they all were. If he had moments of caution, the family all worked together, pulled up their bootstraps and met the challenge head on. At school, Jenna might've been having the best of days, until she wasn't....those moments were especially tough on Jenna. So I would ask her out into the hall so that she could take some gentle time to breathe, and calm herself down with plenty of hugs before she could get on with her day.

Jenna's compassion, grit and humor are such worthy qualities for someone so young. She and Luke shared so much of their humor together. Her compassion comes from the heart and has been within her the whole time. Her grit comes from her parents' ability to put one foot in front of the other to keep going through the trials and tribulations that families face with Duchenne Muscular Dystrophy.

When Luke passed away, it was a very difficult time but the family's strength comes from an undying support of one another. The memorial was well attended by family and friends and the reception was an amazing, true testament of Luke's life. Jenna thoroughly enjoyed the moment with reminders of Luke's amazing life all around her. The family celebrates him daily knowing that while Luke is enjoying absolutely no boundaries; his gift to them includes the freedom for them to wander to many new horizons.

Misty has done an excellent job of writing how the moments in Luke's life affected Jenna and those around her. Jenna misses Luke terribly, but keeps her head high and delves into life looking for kindness and beauty everywhere she can. I smiled a lot when I read Misty's words. Jenna still gives 'everything' a name, takes in life at school, her home, loves her animals and often surprises us with her own simplistic ideas to solve the discussion at hand. Yes, and heart shaped rocks never go unnoticed!

Enjoy this read. It comes from the loving heart of a mom

and a great family I am proud to know.

I anxiously look forward to watching Jenna grow into the amazing young woman I know she will be.

-Kathleen R. Jones
a.k.a. "The Peace Teacher"

*"The most beautiful things in the world*
*cannot be seen or even touched,*
*they must be felt with the heart."*

*~ Helen Keller*

# 1 HEART OF THE MATTER

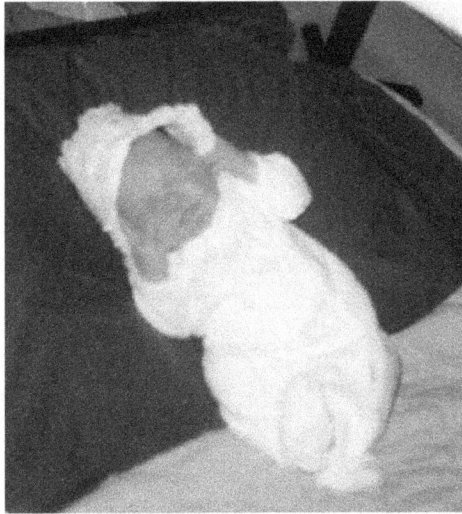

## God wouldn't give me more than I could handle, right?

I used to have this idea that my son being dealt the hand of Duchenne was the end of all my troubles, or at least that no new ones would appear. I believed that somehow I would get through this tragedy, help a bunch of other people in the process, and then get on with life. Yes, it would hurt like hell, but other parents had learned to go on after the death of a child. I figured I'd find a way to survive one way or another. For a while I also bought into the "there's nothing we can do so go home and enjoy your son while you still have him" mentality hook, line and sinker.

The God wouldn't give me more than I could handle saying was almost my mantra. I had absolutely no idea that once you start on the Duchenne journey, you are on the journey for life. Let's just say I didn't get the memo.

# "You're Pregnant."

WHAT? This question screamed in my mind. I knew I hadn't been feeling well, but pregnant? No way was this happening. What was I going to tell Glen? We weren't even married yet. I knew that he hadn't wanted any children of his own; he had told me so. Luke was newly diagnosed with an incurable disease, and worse, this baby could have Duchenne too! I was just sick inside from this news. My friend who was with me at the time later told me I looked like I had just seen a ghost.

All I knew at that moment was that I would keep this baby no matter what. I took the long way home to absorb this new change in my life before springing the news on Glen. I was pretty sure that Luke, who was 7 at the time, would be okay with the news, probably even excited. I also knew I had to be certain in my heart about what I was going to do, no matter what Glen decided.

If you read my first book, In Your Face, you know that Glen chose us, knowing that Luke had Duchenne, knowing there was a possibility the new baby could have Duchenne and all. We got married and committed to create the best life possible for our family. Luke was the ring bearer and both my boys wore mud flaps (what Glen told Luke the tails of their tuxedoes were).

# Little Bird

After the initial shock of actually being pregnant wore off, I had this internal "knowing" the baby I was carrying was a girl. For obvious reasons besides already having a boy, I knew I needed this baby to be a girl. I wasn't so sure I could handle another blow. Her name was already Jenna, which means little bird. I was about 7 months along and even with all the previous ultrasounds, we couldn't tell the sex of the baby. My anxiety was high as I worried that my gut feelings might be wrong. I kept second guessing myself until one spring morning. I had been up all night with worry the night before. I had asked God to give me a sign if I was right about this baby being a girl. I got my answer.

I was getting ready to leave for my last ultrasound after working in our greenhouse that day. And up in the tree was this lone "little bird" singing its heart out. I cried all the way to the ultrasound appointment and when the doctor asked me if I knew the sex of the baby, I said, "She's a girl."

"Are you okay?"

Jenna was born on a sunny July morning. I immediately fell in love with her as she nursed and gazed into my eyes for the very first time. She was the most beautiful baby I'd ever seen. She was an angel. All of a sudden up high on the left side of my body, in the high lung upper throat area, was this intense pain that made me very uncomfortable. I felt like I had swallowed something entirely too big. One nurse asked me if I was okay. I said "Yes, but I have this horrible pain," and I grabbed where the pain was coming from. They whisked Jenna away from me. They gave me a shot of blood thinners and had me hooked up to almost every machine they had. I came to find out I had a pulmonary embolism, which means

I had a blood clot in my lungs. They were very worried the clot would travel either to my brain or my heart. Although I was scared, I had my baby girl, my wonderful husband, and an incredible son with an uncertain future who needed me.

I had found a life I had never dreamed of and I wasn't going anywhere!

# Cheerio O's

We brought her home in a white eyelet lace baby bonnet. Over the next month of newborn-ness Jenna would make these O's with her mouth as she looked around. She was often referred to as pumpkin, turnip, and pickle as each of us had our own vegetable names for her. She was the highlight of our lives, our "little sprout". For her first Halloween we dressed her up as a baby leopard, black nose and all. Then the first Christmas came. We were totally enamored with her.

# Whirlwind

Great Grandma Mary from Texas called Jenna "a little whirlwind" as Jenna ran through the house never missing a beat. And her Great Oma on Glen's side would marvel over how determined she was to learn new things. However, I was starting to notice her not so fun trait of being overly sensitive and whiny over small things. This forced me to change my parenting style since she'd throw a fit from the pressure of not only wanting to do good, but not wanting to do what was expected or being asked. On one hand I knew that being a sensitive person is a gift, but on the other I worried how we were going to handle it as she got older.

# Furniture to Furniture

As most babies do before they start to walk, Jenna found comfort and more freedom going from furniture to furniture. She was thrilled to be standing on her own and taking her first steps. This is also when the progression of her brother's disease started to become more apparent. At 8 years old he reverted to the comfort and safety of going from one piece of furniture to the next. As Jenna started walking, her brother was taking his last steps. We knew the electric wheelchair wasn't too far ahead.

# Brotherly Love

Luke was proud of Jenna; he loved her and continually showed his affection. There wasn't too much jealousy on his part. Maybe it was the years between them. Whatever it was, he felt very protective of her. I'd take him to her doctor's appointments with me. He would watch them like a hawk just waiting for them to mess up. Nobody was going to hurt his baby sister!

# Road Kill

The toddler years – and yes, Luke's first wheelchair – found Jenna wanting to be a part of Luke's every waking moment. She loved riding on the back of his wheelchair and taking whatever Luke was using or playing with and running away. She knew Luke couldn't catch her. She would squeal and run. Luke would get fed up and tell her she was going to be "road kill." There was no way Luke was ever going to hurt her. He was always fearful of running over her anyway. But kids will be kids, and the empty threat was what he had to work with.

## Shared Custody

Luke's dad would come and pick him up for his two weeks. When Jenna was a baby she would cry and cry seeing her brother leave. As his disease progressed, the two weeks turned into a time for doing things her brother physically couldn't, and a time for resting up until he came home again. It was a time for her to be just Jenna.

*"Where so ever you go,
go with all your heart."
~Unknown*

# 2- HAVE A HEART

During these years our main focus was giving Luke the best life we could while living, working, and taking care of his physical needs. There was always a lot of love with a big dose of fear. But we did the best we could, and looking back, probably better than a lot of people do without living in the face of Duchenne Muscular Dystrophy. Jenna was just as swept up in it as we were. It's not like she had a choice, but she never complained and simply accepted that this was her life. She gave her love and support easily and would even put herself on the back burner, not wanting to rock the boat. However, being so young and living such an emotional roller coaster 24/7, her feelings had to come out somehow.

As the toddler years ended, through pre-school and on into grade school Jenna's personality started to emerge. My beautiful, determined whirlwind started to become increasingly volatile and extremely emotional over the littlest things. At one point I remember thinking, *what happened to my little girl?* I was very concerned for her, especially when her classmates started calling her a crybaby. Jenna would still have moments of being her on-purpose self, then with a flip of a switch she became a whiny, crying, hesitant, almost fearful child. In public she'd become a real handful. I could see and feel other mothers pass judgment on her. I was at a loss for how to help my pumpkin pie.

I've heard it said that when there are problems with a child, you should look to the child's home life. The fact was her brother was losing his independence and having to go through surgeries, and would become sick easily. The daily fear of living knowing her brother could die was taking its toll, not just on her but on me. I was torn. I knew we wouldn't have Luke with us forever and I didn't want us as a family to miss one moment. I wanted Jenna to be included all the way. I was plagued with thoughts like *Jenna is just as important as Luke. How am I going to live in fear of losing my son and still be the mother my daughter needs me to be?* Because obviously what I was doing wasn't working.

I decided to do what I always do when I'm backed into a corner. I start asking for a sign telling me what to do. Believe me when I say, I got many of them!

## He Found His Way Back to Her

Jenna loves animals with her whole heart. We already had Max, the family dog, but I felt that Jenna needed a kitty of her very own. So when I heard about free farm kitties up the road it was perfect timing. Having something to love and take care of seemed just the right thing for her. What was even more perfect was that she was able to have the pick of the litter. Jenna's only requirement was that she wanted a girl cat. She picked a cute little friendly fuzzy orange tabby kitty. The owners said it was a girl, but I didn't think orange tabby cats were ever females. I kept quiet until we had to take Kloe to the vet for her first shots. When we came in, the lady at the desk said, "Do you know Kloe is a boy?" I thought, *oh no, time for a meltdown.* Nope, Jenna didn't miss a beat: "Well then his name has to be Ken." The gal and I looked at each other. Jenna put her hand on her hip and said, "You know, Barbie and KEN?" Whew, what a relief. Well, about a month later Ken got out of our van somehow when we were at Luke's physical therapy appointment, about 3 miles from home. We searched all over for him. I was so afraid to tell Jenna that I had lost her cat. I cried all the way home to tell her. Just like I thought, she cried herself to sleep that night, and the next. I felt horrible. On the third night I heard a squeaking sound on the glass patio doors. It was KEN! I couldn't believe it. I scooped him up and put him in bed with Jenna. She was overjoyed that he had found his way back to her.

## Brownies

I was still looking for signs about what I needed to do to help Jenna when she came home wanting to join girl scouts. But there was a catch. There happened to be too many girls and not enough leaders. Here was something Jenna wanted to do and it looked like if I didn't step up and be the leader she wouldn't get to be a part of it. I couldn't let that happen. I remember driving away after signing up to be a girl scout leader thinking, *what did I just do? Okay God, I'm listening. You know with Luke's care I hardly have time for much else.* I was scared and excited all at the same time but I knew this was the sign I needed. I knew Jenna needed to be a part of something outside the home, something just for her. We were already trying ballet, soccer, basketball... nothing was working. But what was different about girl scouts is that Jenna and I were doing it together. Although I had no idea how to be a girl scout leader I had 7 little girls wanting to become brownies. It was fun doing art projects, going on field trips and jamborees. And let's not forget the girl scout cookies. Jenna was still emotional but we were making progress. I could tell she liked me being her girl scout leader. But something still wasn't right. I just couldn't put my finger on it.

## Caregiver Nightmare

Something had happened to my Jenna and her brother that I was unaware of. It didn't come out until the year she joined girl scouts but it reveals more about why my sweet girl was often times an emotional wreck. A care provider of Luke's was terrorizing my children by making them watch bloody scary movies and then she'd lock Jenna in her room. It was horrifying! We were unable to bring charges against the care provider. Jenna went from being able to sleep in the dark to needing a night light and not sleeping well. Luckily this care provider was only in our house a couple of months. However, the damage had been done.

## Her Gift

Starting in preschool and continuing through grade school teachers would tell me how compassionate and helpful Jenna was toward others, and then almost in the same breath they would say – "But we have been dealing with her tears and crying in the class room." After one such meeting when Jenna got into the van, she seemed quiet so I asked her if anything was wrong. Tears instantly sprang to her eyes as she told me that kids on the playground were calling her a crybaby. Just then I had a wave of insight wash over me. I found a safe place to pull over. I told her I was sorry she had to deal with mean kids. I also went on to tell her that being sensitive wasn't all bad. She screamed, "I HATE IT!" I let her have her moment. Then I asked her what was wrong with being sensitive and having a huge heart? What was wrong with wanting to understand and get things right or helping someone else when they are having a hard time? She said nothing. I said, "Maybe, just maybe, you can look at your sensitivity in a new way." She sat up a bit higher and asked, "What way?" I told her she might not know it but having a heart and being sensitive was her gift. I went on to tell her that her only job was learning how to manage all her emotions and overwhelming feelings when they came up. So when she started feeling those tears well up, she should take a deep breath and be patient with herself. I could tell it pleased her deeply to know she wasn't a crybaby, that her heart was her gift. At that moment I realized what Jenna needed most. She needed me.

## Pirates of the Caribbean

When we added a deck to our home Luke and Jenna loved spraying it down with the hose while Luke would prop the broom or squeegee and push the water off. Something about this process and the boards of the deck made them imagine the deck was a pirate ship. I tell this story because it was such a joy for me to watch Jenna interact with Luke. Before she started spraying she would always make sure Luke had the tool he wanted to use all propped up and ready. Nine times out of ten she would let Luke lead the pretend scenario they were playing out. Many times I was taken prisoner until they would get hungry. Being raised alongside Luke, Jenna was able to develop her gift of being sensitive and showing her heart.

## Tinkerbelle Café

I don't think there is a kid out there who doesn't love playing with cardboard boxes. Jenna is no different. Her box creation that stands out the most to me and really shows her creativity and heart is from when we got a new refrigerator. She decided to make a house that served tea. This was how the Tinkerbelle Café was born. She decorated the outside while Glen cut a hole out so she could serve "real" hot tea out the window. I asked her who her customers would be. She said, "Grandma!" We even have a picture of her serving tea to her grandma out the window of the Tinkerbell Café.

## It Stresses Me Out!

Up until this conversation I had with Jenna, I had always brought her with me and Luke to his doctor appointments. She was young and it was just easier to bring her along instead of trying to find a sitter. However, as she got older, I had been thinking about stopping this practice as muscular dystrophy was ravaging Luke's body further. I knew the talk would be heavy and I knew it would be emotionally tough for me. I felt she just didn't need to hear how bad Luke was getting. Little did I know she was already thinking the very same thing. She actually told me she was relieved because in her words, "IT STRESSES ME OUT!" It was incredible to hear her be so aware of herself and her feelings. It was real growth on her part. I did have feelings of brief guilt that I hadn't seen it before, but boy did it feel good to start seeing progress in Jenna handling her feelings. And she even expressed them in a truthful manner.

## The Heart in My Pocket

I am not 100% positive when Jenna found her first heart shaped rock, but I do remember when she gave me my first one. I was standing in security at the airport emptying my pockets because the alarm kept beeping and they wouldn't let me through. I was taking everything out of my pockets and there amongst the coins and one lone earring was a very little heart shaped rock. I was touched so deeply as it was a sign that she was getting from me what she needed. Further, I was delighted that she was showing her love for me.

## Glasses

I asked Jenna why she was squinting at the TV and she said it was because she couldn't see it well. What? How long had this been going on? She wasn't sure... a long time. I couldn't believe it. Here she was after being held back to take 2nd grade over again and it turns out she can't see? It was like, duh! Sure enough, she needed glasses. At first she hated the idea. She cried to me, "But Mom, I'll look stupid." I told her to look at me. I said, "I'm your mom and the last thing I'll let happen is for you to look stupid. I bet we find really pretty glasses to bring out the green in your eyes!" And we did. She has now tried contacts but always goes back to glasses. Somehow I had to make sure she started realizing that she mattered just as much as Luke.

# Peace Teacher

With Jenna as sensitive as she was, I knew her 4th grade teacher needed to be caring but firm, creative but structured enough that Jenna felt supported. It was especially important since Jenna had already been held back and had an Individual Education Plan. Besides having a brother like Luke, she already felt so different and her emotions still often threatened to overwhelm her. This meant her new teacher also needed to be mindful of her issues, without letting Jenna get away with feeling sorry for herself. I was hoping another adult could help Jenna learn new ways of coping, but I was almost certain this was wishful thinking. I went to all the 4th grade teachers' rooms and talked to a few of them. The last classroom I walked into was empty, as the teacher wasn't there yet. I looked around and saw peace signs from all over the world. There was a tree with no leaves but with blown eggs hanging from the branches, and collected rocks lying around here and there. There were newspaper articles tacked up about animals. Whoever this teacher was, I knew she was truly caring, knowledgeable and loved life, just like my Jenna. I instantly knew this was the right teacher for Jenna. Mrs. Jones ended up being the best medicine we could have hoped for. Jenna was lucky enough to have her for 5th grade as well. Even to this day, Mrs. Jones is a support person not only for Jenna but for our entire family. She taught Jenna the very useful technique of taking a moment to collect herself whenever she felt the emotions well up inside her. I see Jenna using this technique often. It makes me so proud she isn't stuffing her feelings down but rather letting them wash through her as needed. I need to internalize that lesson as well.

# No More Bread

The final factor in Jenna's outbursts revealed its ugly head when I had to start picking her up from school because her tummy hurt. We started noticing a bad smell to her breath, and big circles under her eyes. Many nights I'd find her lying on the bathroom floor bloated and miserable. Plus her emotions were in full swing. But the worst thing I noticed was that she was losing weight she didn't have to lose. We had already taken her off dairy so I knew this wasn't her issue. Everything I read about Jenna's symptoms pointed to gluten intolerance. I had been experiencing some symptoms as well so we went off gluten together and we scheduled a doctor's appointment for Jenna in 4 days' time. By the second day off gluten her symptoms were completely gone and I was starting to feel much better as well. We tested her for celiac's disease, which thankfully was negative, and scheduled another appointment for a month down the road. Jenna ended up gaining back 7 pounds in 30 days. And I lost 2 inches from around my waist! It was a challenge going gluten free but we managed, and now we have fun trying new recipes or remaking the really good ones we find.

*"Only from your heart can
you touch the sky."*

*~ Rumi*

# 3- LOVE ROCKS

By this point in Jenna's life Luke was a senior in High School and Jenna was in 5th grade. There was this feeling of, *he made it*. He had made it longer then we were told he would. My Jenna was happy, her grades were coming up. Then Luke got severely sick. We were flung back in the trenches of a great amount of fear, sleep loss, and insurmountable stress. This was one of the scariest blips of time I had ever experienced. It must have been for Jenna too.

## *Don't Die Without Me*

After the Homecoming dance in October 2009, Luke and 300 other students ended up with the swine flu. But since Luke had Duchenne on top of the swine flu, he ended up with pneumonia. So off to the hospital we went; I was pretty sure he would be admitted. We were all scared, knowing this could take Luke's life. I thought we had managed not to alarm Jenna as she seemed to get up and go to school just fine. She appeared to be rolling with the punches. As we were loading the van up to take Luke to the hospital the phone rang and it was Jenna leaving a message. She was crying, telling me to tell Luke, "Don't die without me!" I called her back and told her if things got worse I'd send for her. I promised!

## In Your Face Duchenne Muscular Dystrophy, All Pain, All GLORY!

If you've read my book In Your Face you know Luke made a full recovery and it was this event that inspired me to write it in the first place. I wanted to capture his life's essence while he was still here with me. Little did I know what impact this book about Luke's life would have on the world of Duchenne or even how much of an impression it would make on Jenna, even though she had been in the face of Duchenne Muscular Dystrophy the entire time.

## She Got Her Hug

During the editing and final writing of *In Your Face* I learned about a new electrical stimulation of the nerve treatment called the STS that was already helping boys with Duchenne. When I shared this news with Jenna, including a video of a boy getting stronger, she looked at me and asked, "You mean Luke could hug me back?" I just squeezed her and said, "We will see, I sure hope so!" We knew the treatment wasn't a cure but we were hopeful for any positive results. On the third day of treatment Luke had regained some strength and mobility. He cried to us that he had thought he'd never get to feel good again. And yes, Jenna did get her hug as the photo shows at the beginning of this chapter.

## Victory Bible Camp

When Luke headed to MDA summer camp each summer, Jenna would go to Victory Bible Camp. She always had such great fun with the water sports, craft activities, food, worship songs, and campfires. The summer of 2010 was no different; we had just gotten back from Luke's Texas trip where she got her hug. She was feeling on top of the world. We all were. When her week was finished at camp and I picked her up, she had a big white cross painted on one cheek. She told me it was for Luke.

## Mom, Look!

I went running into her room thinking it was an emergency! When I got in there she was standing with her left leg out holding her pajama bottom up. I was like, WHAT? She was like, LOOK! Still I was clueless, and I could tell by the look she gave me that she thought so too. She had always had this small, peasized, light red blotch of a birthmark on her leg. But, suddenly and beautifully, it had transformed into the shape of a heart! Her entire being radiated delight in her new finding. I thought, *how perfectly fitting for my girl with a HUGE heart.*

*"A kind heart is a fountain of gladness,
making everything in its vicinity
freshen into smiles."
~ Washington Irving*

# 4- *Big Hearted*

Jenna not only finds heart shaped rocks, she's an expert in finding hearts in nature everywhere she goes.

We have heart shaped rocks in every windowsill, in cup holders and pockets, in my purse and on my desk. Jenna gives them to people she cares about all the time. It's her way of saying, "My heart sees the heart in you, and I care." What's so beautiful to see in her is that through all of Luke's surgeries, his life struggle to live with his disease, and all the turmoil she has witnessed the family go through, she has found her own way of being happy. She remains full of love, willing to share it at the drop of a hat. She gives her heart gently, but full on.

She has told me that finding heart shaped rocks is like finding signs that everything is going to be okay.

# Lego Nation

Jenna's dad, Glen, built what we referred to as the Big Table. Basically it was a counter top with four legs, tall enough that Luke could park his wheelchair and prop his hands up on the edge so he and Jenna could play games, before his hands got too weak to build legos together. Before the STS treatment, which is now called the Vecttor, Jenna did most of the building while Luke directed her. They would spend hours building contraptions and playing games together. One day I had run to the store and when I came back, Luke and Jenna were beaming with pride. Jenna said, "His hands are getting stronger!" Luke said, "I built this truck all by myself without assistance from Jenna." This was the beginning of what ended up being Lego Nation filling up half of our living room. When Luke moved out the first time we had to pack up all the buildings, Lego trucks and people so we could put them in our basement. Jenna delicately put each piece into its own labeled bag and carefully placed all the sets together in boxes, also labeled. The idea was for them to build them all back downstairs.

# Gold Mine Conversation

Luke moving out was hard on us all, but it was probably the hardest on me. I experienced empty-nest syndrome coupled with the fact that I was scared out of my mind I'd lose him while he was gone. I hadn't ever really thought he'd move out completely. On one hand, I was thrilled for him, but I knew that things could change in a heartbeat. One of the things that Glen, Jenna, and I did without Luke was to travel to a gold mine in the heart of the Alaskan wilderness. It was a trip that wouldn't be possible for Luke to take with us, but he had moved out and his care was covered. During this trip Jenna and I were walking back to camp when I told her, "I miss Luke." She replied, "I do too." I went on and said, "For the first time Luke feels he can live." She said, "I know." Then I told her how I wanted to be the best mom, the best wife, and to write more books. Jenna stopped and looked at me. She said, "Just one problem with that. You already are the best mom."

## "Was I wanted?"

It seems that Jenna and I have most of our conversations in the car, either on the way to school or after. And this day was no different. She asked me, "Was I wanted?" I responded immediately, "Yes, you were the best surprise ever!" She said, "Surprise?" I said, "Yes, you were wanted, you just weren't planned." I went on to tell her that she is meant to be here in every sense of the word. Her life means something very special and she is my angel. She knew what I meant since I had almost died giving birth to her.

## Middle School Blossom

When Jenna started middle school, I was scared for her. I know how kids can behave toward other kids, and with her being so sensitive I could only imagine Jenna's heart being stepped on all the time. She's had some challenges but overall it's been a delight to see her grow. All her teachers tell me what a joy it is to have her in the school. They say that her caring and compassion are generous. They also love how dedicated she is to doing her class work to the best of her abilities. I notice she often helps those kids that need some extra help. Yes, she has a heart but in no way is she weak. Her spirit is strong and full of grace. She is truly a living example of how we all need to live.

## Orange Crush

Luke had moved out and was trying to live his life with more independence. I didn't know how long this would last for him so I decided that Jenna and I needed a quality mother-daughter trip to Maui. We met up with family there but before we did, we were picking up our small economy car from the car rental when they said we had earned a "free" upgrade to a Jeep with a removable roof. Jenna's eyes got big, she started jumping up and down saying "Can we, can we?!" So of course we ended up driving away in a little orange Jeep she named Orange Crush. We toured around Maui and drove the Hana Highway. We had a ball. It was a time we will never forget. We took numerous pictures of ourselves hanging out the top of Orange Crush. We even found matching Orange Crush T-shirt

## Home Again

When Luke moved back home as an adult, it rocked the boat a bit for Jenna since she had been used to getting all the attention for six months by this point. However, she loved having him back home. Finally there was a brother to talk to again, to play games with again. She would watch Luke play his favorite PlayStation games for hours. She also liked that he could help her with her homework. This time was highly stressful since his health had been compromised further by Duchenne, but we also had times of great fun. We started doing what we called Fiesta Friday every weekend. I would make tacos, and Luke would break out the music which he insisted made my food taste better. We would dance, play, and laugh as a family. We all loved Friday.

## Her Babies

With Jenna's and my gluten sensitivity, I cook with a lot of eggs, and since Jenna loves animals so much, we decided to get some laying hens. When the babies (as she referred to them) arrived, she was over the moon. She took pictures of them all and gave them all egg names. There were Eggy, Sunny, Scrambles, and the favorite, Shelly. Sadly, Shelly didn't make it. When Jenna saw Shelly not moving she cried and cried. Later in the season, after they had all started laying eggs, our new favorite was Sunny. When you came in the coop she'd greet you with a peep and stretch her neck in saying hello. She'd climb up in Jenna's hand and sit. It was so adorable. And then we lost Sunny on Christmas Eve. Again, Jenna cried and cried.

## 13th Birthday

None of us could believe Jenna was becoming a teenager. The theme she chose was a hippie peace sign birthday party. We had so much fun. One of the things Jenna does before she opens each gift is to read out loud each birthday card. Before she could read well, she made me do it. I've always found this so endearing. It really shows how much she cares about people and how she likes to make everyone feel good. This time, the card that choked her (and everyone) up was the card from Luke.

TO MY SISTER,
WHO KNOWS ME – WHO I AM,
WHAT I THINK, HOW I FEEL, AND LOVES ME INSIDE
AND OUT…
WHO LAUGHS ME OUT OF MY TOO SERIOUS
MOMENTS, TALKS ME THROUGH THE ONES THAT
REALLY MATTERAND STANDS BY MY SIDE ALLTHE
WAY …
MY SISTER WHOSE HEART IS SO WARM, WHOSE
CARING MEANS SO MUCH, WHO'S LOVED IN SO
MANY WAYS…
HAPPY BIRTHDAY TO MY REALLY SPECIAL SISTER.
LOVE, LUKE

## Walks with Luke

From the time Jenna was born, Luke and I would take walks
with her. As she grew and he ended up in his wheelchair full
time this practice didn't change. When she was small she'd ride
on the back of his wheelchair. She loved being with him. As
they grew up, the walks evolved into time they'd spend taking
pictures  of our beautiful Alaskan mountains, animals, and
scenery. They'd spend hours outside pretending and just
being brother and sister. I loved watching them outside
together, seemingly without a stress in the world.

## Love at First Sight

Out of the eleven pups left none of them seemed just right
for my Jenna. They were all cute, as puppies are, but we didn't
see "the one." I could tell that many of them would be real
handfuls to raise properly, and I wanted a dog that Jenna
could handle well. We were about to leave when I saw a smaller
pup, probably  the runt of the litter, buried in a blanket and
fast asleep. I asked the owner if we could see her. She said,
"Sure, but this one is the runt." As she picked her up to hand
her to Jenna, Jenna immediately lifted the pup to look at her,

and the pup opened her eyes and sniffed Jenna's nose. Jenna's look said it all. It was love at first sight for both Jenna and her new puppy, Josie.

*"The heart that truly loves, never forgets."*

# 5- THE HEART WITHIN

Luke had moved out and moved back in and then moved into his very own home within one year. A lot of things happened in a very short period of time, and six months after Luke moved into his own home, his untimely death hit us out of nowhere. Duchenne had weakened his body to the point where he couldn't fight any more.

Living on his own was an accomplishment we all played an important role in. Jenna was a huge help to her brother and looked forward to the time she got to spend with him in his new home.

## Keeping House

When Luke moved back, his plan was to find a place of his own that we'd help him manage his life from. It was very important for him to have as much independence as he possibly could. On move-in day Jenna was so excited for him. She helped him decorate and set it all up. Once it was all set up she went over on Sunday afternoons for game day. Then I'd bring dinner and we'd all eat together.

## Beach Dream

"Mom, did I tell you about my beach dream I had the other night?" I said no. "Well, Luke and I were at the beach and it was almost dark. The stars had just starting coming out when Luke got up and started walking toward a light. He turned back towards me and smiled and walked into the light." Then she said, "I was so happy for him." When she was telling me the dream it occurred to me that it might be a premonition, but I pushed that thought swiftly from my mind. I focused on listening to her. She told me she took the dream as a sign that everything was going to be okay.

## Cloudy Cold Day

As Luke was lying in the hospital taking his last breaths of life, the minutes rolled into hours. It was a bitter cold dreary day with the clouds rolling in, covering Luke's mountains that we could see from his 2nd floor room. Jenna would come into the room for a few minutes, then leave again, unreadable without saying anything. I was so worried for my family, for myself. Would Luke pull out of this? I thought not. On one of her trips into the room I said to Luke that his room had a great view but that clouds had covered his mountains. This must have made an impression on Jenna because the next time she came in the room, she taped up a picture she had drawn on lined paper of the sun coming out over the mountains. She had written underneath. "I BROUGHT YOU YOUR MOUNTAINS BACK.

Love, Jenna.

## For My Brother

We all wanted to put something special in Luke's casket to be buried with him. We all gathered individual items that we wanted. The first thing Jenna added was all the "gotcha rocks" we'd gathered over the years. Gotcha rocks were the little rocks Luke's wheelchair brought into the house that we stepped on. He would always say "Gotcha!" when we did. Then Jenna went to her room and found the most perfect heart shaped rock to go with him.

# Epilogue

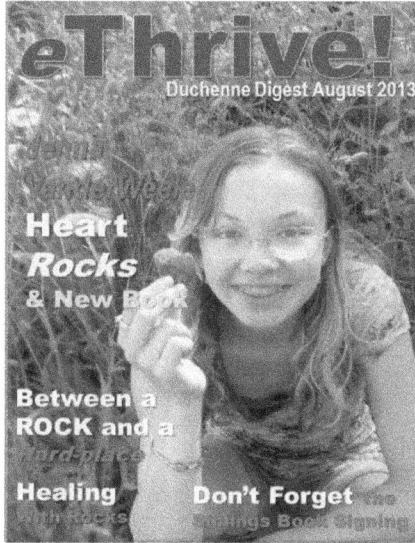

eThrive!
Duchenne Digest August 2013

Heart
Rocks
& New Book

Between a
ROCK and a

Healing          Don't Forget

## Living Life Through
## Jenna-Colored Glasses

One day not long ago, I was telling Jenna how neat it was
for her to be achieving the good grades she has been getting
and how well she seems to be doing, especially since grieving
her brother hasn't been easy. She told me, "It's probably
because I'm not worried anymore. I miss him, but I am not
worried."

We have heart shaped rocks in every windowsill, in cup
holders and pockets, in my purse and on my desk. Jenna gives
them to people she cares about all the time. It is her way of

saying, "My heart sees the heart in you, and I care." What's incredibly beautiful for me to witness about Jenna is that through all of Luke's surgeries, his life struggle living a disease, his death, all the grief, and the crazy turmoil she has witnessed and gone through personally, she has found her own way of being happy and full of love, and she is willing to share it at the drop of a hat. She gives her heart gently, but full on.

"If she's crying, don't say anything. Just hug her."

On any given day, no matter the season, you can send Jenna out to find a heart shaped rock and she'll come back more times than not with more than one. She has told me that finding heart shaped rocks is like finding signs that everything is going to be okay. They are there just for her to find.

Jenna's
Heart Shaped Rock
Finding Recipe:

*"Let go of it having to be a perfect shaped heart, because rocks are like people. We are all different and none of us are perfect."*

# Who is
# Misty VanderWeele

I am a fun-loving mom, wife, and friend who is learning to live and thrive through the heartache of grief I feel from the death of my son, Luke. It has not been easy. However, I know I MUST keep living through the tears anyway. Life is meant to be LIVED, full on, with hope, faith, and passion.

I am known for my Duchenne Muscular Dystrophy Advocacy work through the books I write, my e-magazine, website, and blog. I'm committed to sharing the Duchenne story until the whole world hears. My recent findings about Nutrition and Muscular Dystrophy will bring another level of understanding as I believe without a doubt our answers and cures for disease lies within Nutrition. I have proof to back it up too.

Shortly after publishing the first book I wrote for my son about his disease Duchenne entitled *In Your Face Duchenne Muscular Dystrophy All Pain All GLORY!* I knew I wanted to write my daughter a book too. Tucking this idea in my hat I went on to compile three more books of Duchenne stories from around the world, *Saving Our Sons, Saving Our Sons and Daughters II and Don't Forget the Siblings.*

Heart Shaped Rocks is the second piece of my personal Duchenne journey in that it details the experience through my daughter's life. It documents how Duchenne has helped mold her into an incredible young lady who always looks for the beauty around her.

On my website www.MistyVanderWeele.com I invite you to unlock all the resources I have compiled, including a free e-book titled *Love, Light and Strength* and the free eThrive Duchenne Digest. You can also join the TNC (Thrive Network Community) for even more support, coping techniques, and a how to advocate video series.

# *About the Editor*

## Lucia Craven of Craven Review

Craven Review offers editorial expertise with over 10 years of experience crafting a variety of finely honed written works. I have drafted and edited countless writing projects, including essays, articles, blogs, newsletters, business plans, fiction, poetry, curricula, and research.

I am a freelance editor, writer, and teacher currently living in North Carolina with my husband and young son. I hold a Bachelor's degree in English from Wesleyan University and a Master of Arts in Teaching secondary English education from Columbus State University, where I graduated with honors. With years of experience teaching high school and directing academic programs, I am a stickler for clarity, precision, and polish. Drawing on my educational background, I proofread and revise with ease, expediency, and the highest of standards. In addition to editorial work, I have written science and literary materials for classroom texts and authored web text for various educational institutions.

I am thrilled to add Heart Shaped Rocks to my collection of edited pieces. It is a heartwarming memoir of family, growth, grief, and, most of all, love. It is impossible to read without being moved, and that is what makes it truly a gift from the heart.

IN **Your** **Face**

Duchenne Muscular Dystrophy
...All Pain...All GLORY!

Misty VanderWeele

**Duchenne Muscular Dystrophy** wasn't going to stop this mom from living the best life possible. Misty shares openly the roller-coaster of Duchenne in this heart touching, surprisingly laugh provoking  book about her son, Luke, *In Your Face Duchenne Muscular Dystrophy All Pain All Glory!*

## 98 Heart Touching Personal Stories
## Shinning the LIGHT on Duchenne Muscular Dystrophy

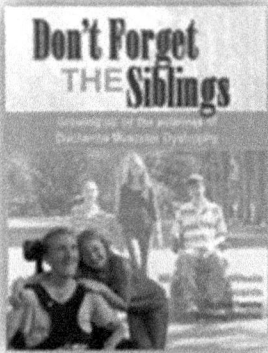

**Don't Forget the Siblings,** Duchenne parent and sibling stories about living in the face of Duchenne Muscular Dystrophy

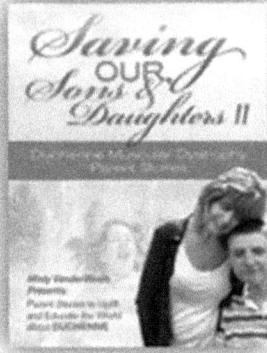

**Duchenne** affects daughters too! *Saving Our Sons & Daughters II* includes real life stories from Parents, Siblings and those afflicted with Duchenne. They tell their stories knowing education is "key" to finding a cure!

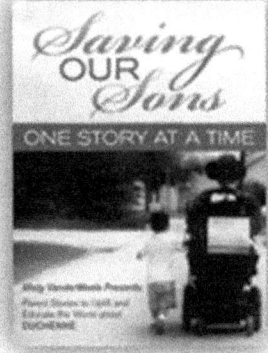

*Saving Our Sons One Story at a Time,* First Duchenne-Parent collaboration book of its kind. Where parents come together to share their personal stories as a way to shout out their SOS call to the WORLD, that *A CURE MUST BE FOUND!*

www.ingramcontent.com/pod-product-compliance
Lightning Source LLC
Chambersburg PA
CBHW032033090426
42741CB00006B/801